21st
Century
Skills Library

LIFE SKILLS BIOGRAPHIES

MADAM C. J. WALKER

Katie Marsico

Cherry Lake Publishing
Ann Arbor, Michigan

CHERRY LAKE Publishing

Published in the United States of America by Cherry Lake Publishing
Ann Arbor, MI
www.cherrylakepublishing.com

Content Adviser: Page Putnam Miller, PhD, Visiting Distinguished Lecturer in the
Department of History, University of South Carolina, Columbia, South Carolina

Photo Credits: Cover and pages 1, 10, 23, 24, 26, 29, 30, 32, 34, 39, and 42, Madam C. J.
Walker Collection, Indiana Historical Society; pages 5, 7, 9, 13, 18, 20, 37, and 41, Photo
courtesy of Library of Congress; page 14, © Corbis; page 17, General Research and
Reference Division, Schomburg Center for Research in Black Culture, The New York
Public Library, Astor, Lennox and Tilden Foundations; page 40, A'Lelia Bundles/Walker
Family Collection/madamcjwalker.com

Library of Congress Cataloging-in-Publication Data
Marsico, Katie, 1980-
 Madam C.J. Walker / by Katie Marsico.
  p. cm. — (Life skills biographies)
 ISBN-13: 978-1-60279-074-2 (hardcover)
 ISBN-10: 1-60279-074-4 (hardcover)
 1. Walker, C. J., Madam, 1867-1919—Juvenile literature. 2. Cosmetics industry—United States—
History—Juvenile literature. 3. African American women executives—Biography—Juvenile
literature. I. Title. II. Series.
 HD9970.5.C672W35596 2008
 338.7'66855092—dc22
 [B]   2007004438

Cherry Lake Publishing would like to acknowledge the work of
The Partnership for 21st Century Skills.
Please visit www.21stcenturyskills.org for more information.

CONTENTS

INTRODUCTION

At a time when African Americans faced a world filled with **discrimination** and few opportunities, Madam C. J. Walker proved that faith, hard work, and determination can lead to success. A self-made businesswoman, Walker used her beauty and hair care products to build a remarkable personal fortune. This child of former slaves never stopped giving back to the community and never lost her drive to end the violence and **segregation** that other African Americans had to endure. Her personal progress became an inspiration to people of all races, as well as a tool for social change.

CHAPTER ONE

HARD TIMES AND A HARD WORKER

Cotton plantations were common in the South in the 1800s.

Madam C. J. Walker was born Sarah Breedlove on December 23, 1867, in Delta, Louisiana. Her parents, Owen and Minerva Breedlove, were former slaves who already had four children—Louvenia, Owen Jr., Alexander, and James. Minerva also gave birth to a fourth son, Solomon, in 1869.

Young Sarah labored in the cotton fields alongside her parents. Pulling the cotton from its seed pod made Sarah's fingers raw and bloody, and the constant bending to pick the plants hurt her back. But Sarah worked as hard as she could to help her family. At a very early age, Sarah learned the importance of being responsible for herself.

Sarah was born only two years after the Civil War (1861–1865) ended and the Thirteenth Amendment to the U.S. Constitution was ratified. This amendment put an end to slavery in the United States, but life was still difficult for African Americans like Sarah and her family. People of color still faced discrimination and struggled to receive fair treatment, especially when it came to finding new jobs. The Breedloves continued working on their former master's plantation as **sharecroppers**, which meant that they paid the plantation owner for use of the land with a portion of the cotton they grew.

Like many African American sharecroppers, Sarah's parents worked long hours in the cotton fields and didn't make much money for their efforts. Sometimes Sarah's mother washed other people's laundry for extra income. The family home had only one room, with a dirt floor, and offered little escape from Louisiana's blistering heat and humidity. In many ways, the Breedloves' life hadn't changed much since they officially gained freedom in 1863.

But African Americans had few options for earning a living so soon after the Civil War. Not only was it nearly impossible to find the same career opportunities as whites, but many African

Washing laundry by hand was hard and tiring work.

Americans who tried to better themselves were frequently harassed, whipped, or **lynched**. Lynching usually involved mobs of white men killing someone by hanging that person. Lynch mobs took the law into their own hands when they decided that someone—often an African American—had done something wrong. In the South at that time, members of lynch mobs generally went unpunished for their actions. They used fear to control African Americans and discourage them from trying for better jobs, having a voice in politics, and getting a quality education.

While some schools were established in Louisiana for African American children, they were not popular with local whites. White farmers worried about who would harvest their crops if their former slaves were busy with classes or finding jobs more suited to someone with a higher education. Many whites feared the power that education would give African Americans, and white teachers who dared to instruct other races were often the victims of violence. With little opportunity for schooling, and because the Breedloves needed her help on the farm, Sarah probably had only about three months of formal education as a child. But her time in the cotton fields taught her the value of hard work and perseverance, even if it came at the price of cracked hands and an aching back.

FORCED TO OVERCOME TRAGEDY

When Sarah was about six, her mother became sick and died. Her father passed away two years later.

Because she was still so young, it wasn't practical for Sarah to try to support herself. She ended up moving to Vicksburg, Mississippi, with her sister, Louvenia, and her brother-in-law, Jesse Powell. Vicksburg was filled with several stately homes as well as shops selling colorful dresses, hats, and shoes that caught the little girl's eye. The southern city offered Sarah a glimpse of wealth and elegance, but her home environment was harsh and unhappy.

Powell wasn't pleased that Sarah was staying with them, and he was often cruel to the young orphan. Sarah's brothers didn't live close by, so she had no other family members to turn to when Louvenia's house became unbearable. To escape Powell's unkindness, Sarah married Moses McWilliams when she was fourteen years old. The couple's only child, Lelia, was born when Sarah was seventeen.

Sarah first glimpsed expensive fashions in Vicksburg, Mississippi.

21st Century Content

Jesse Powell expected Sarah to earn income for his family from the time she was about ten years old. She began doing other people's laundry, using pots of boiling water and a wooden washtub. She pressed clothes with a heavy iron. Sarah had to be careful not only for her own safety but also because a mistake such as burning a customer's shirt meant less money. To be a successful washerwoman, Sarah learned to implement good business practices.

Sarah was widowed when she was 20 years old.

McWilliams, like many African Americans in the late 1800s, took whatever employment was available, including labor for railroads, steamboats, and farms. Sarah divided her time between caring for Lelia and doing other people's laundry for extra money, working tirelessly to provide for her family.

Unfortunately, in 1888, McWilliams died. The exact circumstances of his death are unclear, but many people suspect that he was lynched or involved in a race **riot**. Suddenly left alone with little money and a small child to care for, Sarah was undoubtedly frightened, but she remained driven to find a better life for them both.

Vicksburg, like much of the South, offered Sarah little opportunity. As both a woman and an African American, she knew it would be impossible to escape the poverty and almost constant discrimination there. And the South remained an often dangerous place for African Americans. Not willing to accept this kind of existence for Lelia or herself, Sarah took her daughter and headed for a new future in Saint Louis, Missouri.

CHAPTER TWO

A City of Opportunities

In 1890, Saint Louis was home to more than 450,000 people.

By 1889, Sarah and Lelia had arrived in Saint Louis by steamboat. The city was filled with factories, railroads, and second chances for African Americans looking to escape the dangers and discrimination of the South. Three of Sarah's brothers—Alexander, James, and Solomon—already lived there and worked as barbers. While African Americans were often treated

unfairly in Saint Louis, they still had opportunities to establish themselves within the community and earn better money.

Sarah and Lelia rented a cramped apartment in one of the city's poorer sections, and they were quickly welcomed into the neighborhood and into the Saint Paul African Methodist Episcopal Church. The church offered Sarah a place to pray, and its members provided friendship and assistance. They told Sarah about the Saint Louis Colored Orphans Home. While Lelia wasn't technically an orphan, the home's founders convinced Sarah that her daughter could benefit from spending time in their care and attending classes with other residents at Dessalines Elementary School. Because Sarah had not been able to enjoy a formal education in Louisiana, and since she was working hard as a washerwomen, she was grateful for any help the Orphans Home could offer.

While Sarah's new friends and the generous spirit at Saint Paul's were comforting, her life remained difficult. Like other washerwomen in the late 1800s, she washed clothes by hand. At that time, soap contained an ingredient called lye, which burned Sarah's skin. For all her efforts, she probably earned between $4 and $12 a week and was often forced

In the 1890s, most schools were still segregated.

to move when the rent was raised too high. Despite these hardships Sarah continued to ponder what she could do to achieve a better, more comfortable future for both herself and Lelia.

But challenges remained in the present too. In 1893, Sarah's oldest brother, Alexander, died. About a year later, Sarah married a second time. Unfortunately, her husband, John Davis, did not share her appreciation

Lelia attended college in Knoxville, Tennessee, in the early 1900s.

for hard work. He seemed to have no interest in helping her and Lelia improve their lives. When he wasn't drinking, Davis did little to bring in extra money for his new family, and he was often cruel to his wife and stepdaughter.

Fearful of the influence Davis's behavior would have on her child, Sarah pushed harder than ever for Lelia to have a proper education. She saw to it that the schoolgirl missed as few classes as possible and made sure that she was always dressed presentably in clean clothes. By 1902, Sarah's determination paid off. Much to her satisfaction, she had saved enough money to send Lelia to Knoxville College, in Knoxville, Tennessee.

TURNING INWARD

With Lelia continuing her education, Sarah was finally able to focus more on improving her own situation. She left Davis in 1903 and started seeing a newspaperman named Charles Joseph "C. J." Walker. Unlike Davis, Walker believed in hard work and took pride in being well dressed and having a neat, clean appearance. Perhaps most important, he respected Sarah and her determination to make a better life for herself. Not everyone during this period felt that women should pursue careers outside of the home, so it was satisfying for Sarah to finally meet a man who showed her encouragement instead of cruelty.

Sarah began attending evening classes at local schools to make up for the formal learning she never had as a child. And even though work and school kept her busy, she never forgot the generosity and kindness that the people of Saint Louis had showed

In 1904, Sarah read a newspaper story about an elderly African American man who had to take care of a blind sister and a sick wife. She threw a party to collect money and groceries for the family. It was in Saint Louis that Sarah first recognized her social responsibility and began demonstrating her skills as a **philanthropist**, someone who uses his or her time and money to assist others.

her upon her arrival. She gradually became more active in the community and joined church clubs that aided the less fortunate, often taking it upon herself to raise money for the poor or sick.

Sarah took satisfaction in her work with the church and was recognized as a leader within her own neighborhood, but she was troubled about her future. For several years, she had worried about what would happen when she got older and could no longer handle the physical demands of the laundry business. She wondered to herself, "What are you going to do when you grow old and your back gets stiff? Who is going to take care of your little girl?" But she couldn't see how she, "a poor washerwoman, was going to better [her] condition."

A NEW CAREER

Apart from her future, Sarah's concerns included her hair, which had started falling out in the mid-1890s. Many African American women during this period had the same difficulty. Some didn't wash their hair frequently enough, and others tried treatments that actually did more harm than good. Because people at that time didn't know as much about proper nutrition and health care as they do today, poor diet may also have caused hair to fall out or break more easily. To conceal these problems, African American women often wore head wraps.

Like C. J. Walker, Sarah took great pride in her appearance. She always made sure that she and Lelia wore clean clothes and looked neat and presentable, even though they rarely had money for new dresses or fancy hats and shoes. So Sarah was not satisfied with letting her hair fall out and

Annie Turnbo (above) hired Sarah as a door-to-door saleswoman in 1903.

simply hiding the problem under a head wrap. She experimented with remedies on and off for years but with little success. Then she turned to Wonderful Hair Grower, a hair care product developed by an African American businesswoman named Annie Turnbo.

Sarah went to work as a door-to-door saleswoman for Turnbo starting in 1903. In addition to hoping that her use of the product would ultimately improve her hair, Sarah saw her new career as a definite advancement. As a washerwoman, she "seldom could make more than $1.50 a day," and, as she recalled, "I got my start by giving myself a start." It also was probably rewarding to be employed by a self-made African American businesswoman who had overcome life challenges not unlike Sarah's to become an **entrepreneur**.

Turnbo was likely one of many African Americans who inspired Sarah during this time in her life. In 1904, Saint Louis hosted a World's Fair and was the site of speeches by successful African Americans including poet Paul Laurence Dunbar, author and historian W. E. B. DuBois, and educator

The National Association of Colored Women encouraged women to push for a better education and to break into the 20th century world of **industry**, where people were gaining fame and wealth by creating new, exciting products and services every day. The organization showed Sarah the ability of strong leadership to inspire people and create change.

In 1904, Saint Louis hosted a World's Fair, and people from around the world flocked to the city.

Booker T. Washington. Sarah was also inspired by Washington's wife, Margaret Murray Washington, who helped lead the National Association of Colored Women (NACW). The NACW fought for women's voting rights and worked to end discrimination. Its members were often well-known, accomplished

African American women who used their influence to oppose lynching and laws that denied equal rights to people of color. The NACW, with its slogan "Lifting as We Climb," gave hope to Sarah and others.

Sarah found motivation in the wisdom of the NACW and the words of the famous African American scholars and leaders who passed through Saint Louis. In the nearly sixteen years since her arrival in Missouri, Sarah had survived personal tragedy, poverty, and the challenges of raising a child on her own. But, just as she had seen a future for herself outside of cotton fields and washtubs, her life was about to move beyond selling someone else's product door-to-door.

Still struggling with her own hair loss, Sarah prayed to God to keep from going completely bald. She claimed the response to her prayer was "a dream, and in that dream a big black man appeared to me and told me what to mix for my hair. Some of the remedy was from Africa, but I sent for it, mixed it, put it on my scalp and in a few weeks my hair was coming in faster than it had ever fallen out." Whether she was actually inspired by a dream or simply experimented with Turnbo's Wonderful Hair Grower to come up with her own version of the beauty product, she managed to correct her hair loss. From there, Sarah launched herself on a career path filled with greater wealth, fame, and opportunity than she had ever thought possible.

CHAPTER THREE

BECOMING A BUSINESSWOMAN

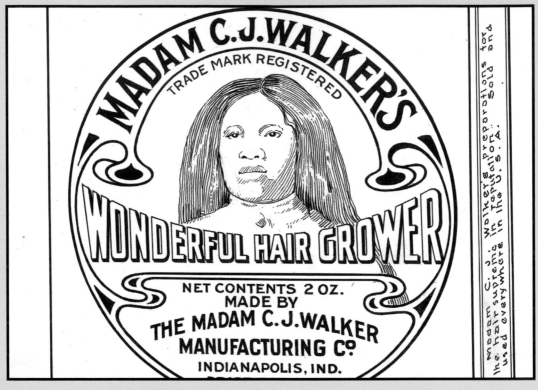

Sarah spent a lot of time experimenting with different ingredients for her hair remedy before she found a recipe that worked.

When Sarah created the mixture that finally put an end to her hair problems, she didn't initially plan on selling it. To her, it was simply a solution that saved her from baldness. Eventually, however, she shared the scalp **ointment** with some of her friends, who found that it worked on their hair too. Sarah began to realize that her homemade beauty product had the potential to be popular with more than a few women in her Saint

Louis neighborhood. She finally saw a way to go into business for herself. Best of all, she knew her product would help African American women feel better about themselves.

But Saint Louis wasn't the right place for Sarah to begin **marketing** her ointment. Missouri was already home to Turnbo and her line of hair care products. Denver, Colorado, appealed to Sarah because it was where her sister-in-law Lucy Breedlove Crockett resided. Because Lelia was still in school, Sarah hoped that Crockett and her four daughters would help give her the fresh start she needed. So, in July 1905, she took a train to the western city, which was famous for its silver mines, ranches, and railroad tracks.

Even though Sarah was determined to form her own business, she was also practical and understood that her dreams wouldn't come true overnight. She continued to sell Turnbo's products, cook, and take in laundry for extra money while perfecting her ointment. Working out of a rented attic, Sarah experimented with ingredients that probably included coconut oil, beeswax, sulfur, and violet extract. She got to know the people in her neighborhood and eventually visited several of their homes to let them try out her scalp treatment. As Sarah later remembered, "I began of course in a most modest way. I [went] house-to-house . . . among people of my race, and after a while I got going pretty well."

When Sarah visited customers' homes, she first shampooed their hair. Next, she added ointment to their hair and scalp. She probably worked with Turnbo's formula at first but likely began to use her own mixture more often as time passed. After applying the hair grower, Sarah rubbed oil on her customers' hair and smoothed it back with a heated steel comb. She later

named this multistep process the Walker System. After she finished the treatment, the women's hair was shiny and straight, and they were relieved to know that they had done something to prevent baldness. As much as she was pleased with the extra money she made, she was equally happy to help other African American women become more confident.

Through her church in Denver, Shorter Chapel African Methodist Episcopal Church, Sarah became acquainted with local African American newspapermen who helped her advertise the sale of Turnbo's products. While Sarah was excited about the idea of marketing her ointment, she wasn't ready to formally strike out on her own yet.

As Sarah worked toward independence as an entrepreneur, C. J. Walker decided to join her in Denver. He arrived in late 1905, and the two were married in January 1906. Almost immediately, her husband began building a career in the real estate and entertainment industries. The couple soon moved to a more comfortable apartment, and it wasn't long before they gained a reputation for giving fancy dinners and parties. Sarah soon began calling herself Madam C. J. Walker in newspaper ads, hoping to convey high quality by including

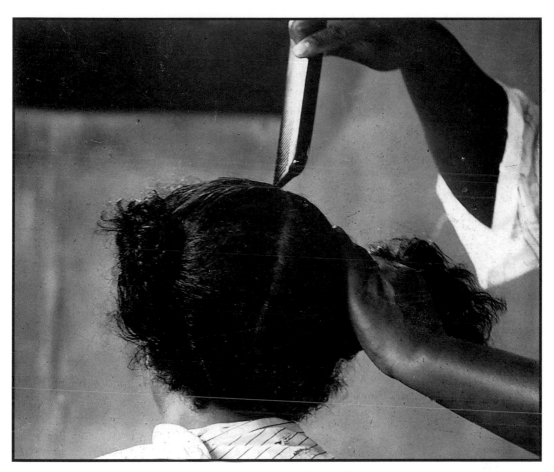

*One of the several steps in the Walker system
included combing the client's hair.*

the polite form of address. She was quickly becoming recognized as an important and elegant member of African American society in Denver.

By mid-1906, Madam C. J. Walker had experienced enough success trying out her own scalp treatments in Colorado that she decided it was time to stop selling for Turnbo. In July of that year, she started traveling across the state to demonstrate the effectiveness of Madam Walker's Wonderful Hair Grower.

One of the ways Walker marketed her products was through advertisements.

EXPANDING ACROSS THE COUNTRY

Walker was thrilled to discover that her formula for hair growth proved popular far beyond Denver's borders. After visiting cities such as Pueblo, Trinidad, and Colorado Springs, she regularly received letters from all over the state requesting that she demonstrate her scalp treatment. In August 1906, Walker was delighted to have Lelia join her in Denver. The two women worked together to mix and ship Madam Walker's Wonderful Hair Grower. They also continued giving scalp treatments to local customers who arrived at their quarters at 2317 Lawrence Street.

Not surprisingly, Turnbo was not pleased with her western competition, and she sent more sales agents to Denver. But Walker already had a mind to move, and she was busily recruiting her own sales agents. In September 1906, she left Lelia in charge of the Denver operation and headed to nearby states to market her hair grower. She saw even greater opportunities in other parts of the country with larger African American populations. So, in 1907, Madam Walker, her husband, and Lelia traveled through Oklahoma, Texas, Kansas, Arkansas, Louisiana, Mississippi, and Alabama.

During these trips, Walker busily met with African American churches and organizations to arrange presentations. She also taught classes for prospective sales agents. Everywhere she went, she received more and more orders for Madam Walker's Wonderful Hair Grower. That year, Walker earned $3,652. In the early 1900s, this was an impressive salary for a white man with a formal education, let alone an African American woman who had grown up picking cotton and washing clothes.

While the Walkers and Lelia were on the road, they likely sent their orders to C. J. Walker's sister, who was also a sales agent. She lived in Louisville,

Learning & Innovation Skills

During presentations and classes, Walker used terms and examples that her audience—mostly women who had left jobs on farms to become her sales agents—would understand. "Do you realize that it is as necessary to cultivate the scalp to grow hair as it is to cultivate the soil to grow a garden?" she once asked. Walker knew it was important to explain concepts within a context her students would understand.

Kentucky, and probably sent shipments from a temporary office there. Sarah realized that this system could not support the number of requests that continued to pour in. Pittsburgh, Pennsylvania, offered the railroads she needed to move her hair grower across the country. Between late 1907 and early 1908, the Walkers bought a house in one of the wealthier sections of Pittsburgh that was also home to many whites. Walker opened her hair parlor in a different part of the city, however, to be near her African American clients.

Using the same determination and charm that had been so effective in Saint Louis and Denver, Walker was tireless in her efforts to meet African American leaders, church officials, and popular figures in Pittsburgh

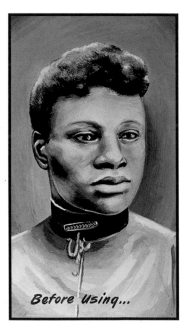

Before treatment, Walker's hair was short and brittle.

society. Her work paid off—community leaders "found her to be a strictly honest, thorough-going businesswoman."

In 1908, Walker earned nearly twice as much as the previous year, and she took on hundreds of new sales agents. In addition, she printed advertisements that showed pictures of her before and after treatment. Walker's long, luxurious, well-groomed hair in the later photograph was enough proof for African Americans around the country. Women who saw the advertisement wanted to try her hair grower and work as her employees. Besides having outward beauty, she symbolized the possibility of success for those who had started out like her.

CREATING JOBS AND SPARKING CONTROVERSY

Up until now, Walker had mainly trained sales agents by offering demonstrations and classes as she traveled around the country. Then, in 1908, she and Lelia opened Lelia College in Pittsburgh, which allowed Walker and her team to instruct an even larger number of African American women. For students who didn't live near Pittsburgh, she provided a **correspondence class** for $25 that taught the Walker System through materials sent by mail.

By training these women, whom Walker referred to as "hair culturists," she was showing them how to achieve independence and finally be rewarded for their hard work. Walker knew from her own life experiences that far too many African American women endured backbreaking labor for most of their lives and still remained poor. They faced discrimination because of both their race and their gender, and most had jobs washing,

Learning & Innovation Skills

Many African American businessmen didn't consider Walker and her workers to be their professional equals. As she noted, these men "were prone to look down upon 'hair dressers' as they called us. . . . So I had to go down and dignify this work." Walker regularly attended conferences and meetings sponsored by African American business leagues. Her ability to communicate the importance of her industry helped her ultimately succeed in reshaping the opinions of many notable African American men, including Booker T. Washington.

cooking, or cleaning for whites. Lelia College and Walker's desire to help other people gave them a way out. She "made it possible for many [African American] women to abandon the wash-tub for more pleasant and profitable occupation."

It didn't take long for Walker to realize that it was time to expand yet again. In early 1910, she arranged for Lelia to handle her Pittsburgh branch and then headed to Indianapolis, Indiana. The state capital was home to a large African American population and, like Pittsburgh, was crisscrossed with railways. Walker wasted no time buying property, including a large brick home, and began building a factory to manufacture her product. With the help of African American newspaperman George Knox, she advertised scalp treatments for 50¢, which was the same price she gave for tins of her hair grower. She also began offering new products and services, including a vegetable shampoo, hair oil called Glossine, various ointments, and manicures.

Business was booming, and Walker needed experts to advise her about money because she was constantly taking steps to train new hair culturists, produce more hair grower, and open a greater number of salons and schools. She therefore hired

When Walker arrived in Indianapolis, one of the first things she did was to have a factory built.

two African American attorneys—Freeman Briley Ransom and Robert Lee Brokenburr—to assist her in managing the business. In 1911, she officially created the Madam C. J. Walker Manufacturing Company.

Much to Walker's satisfaction, Lelia had by this time joined her in Indianapolis. The young woman had been married in Pittsburgh, but the union quickly resulted in divorce. Sadly, Walker's own marriage ended the same way in 1912. She remained focused in spite of her disappointment. In her eyes, financial success didn't mean she could stop working hard. She therefore continued traveling around the country to promote her

Many African American women benefited from attending classes to become hair culturists.

hair grower and to offer training and job opportunities to other African American women. Among these women were Walker's nieces and her older sister, Louvenia.

But no matter how many people Walker's business helped, it still managed to stir up mixed emotions within the African American community. Many African American women's hair was naturally curly, and the Walker System straightened it. A few religious leaders questioned why Walker was trying to make African Americans look different than God had intended. These men suggested that she was attempting to sell an image of white beauty, as white women typically had straighter hair.

Walker responded by emphasizing that she merely hoped to help women's hair grow better and that it was not her goal to straighten it. She explained that she wanted to teach African Americans to take better care of their hair, but that she was in no way trying to detract from their natural beauty. As she said years later, "I have always held myself out as a hair culturist. I grow hair. . . . I have absolute faith in my mission. I want . . . my people to take a greater pride in their appearance and to give their hair proper attention."

Regardless of any controversy, however, things only continued to improve for Walker. In October 1912, Lelia formally adopted a 13-year-old girl named Mae, who was immediately adored by her new mother and grandmother. By the spring of 1913, Walker was making more than $3,000 a month. That same year, she added to her real estate holdings: she bought an elegant home on 136th Street in New York City. For a woman who once found it difficult to make her rent payments in the poorer section of Saint Louis, it was no small thing to own property in one of the wealthier areas of New York. But Walker did not sit back and spend all her hard-earned money on herself and her family. More determined than ever, she used her growing fortune to help other members of her race overcome discrimination and realize success.

CHAPTER FOUR

DETERMINED TO DO MORE GOOD

Walker (in driver's seat) could afford the finest luxuries of the time.

Between 1913 and 1916, Walker didn't rest much, even though she finally had the means to relax and enjoy luxuries that she never could have afforded in the past. Though she did treat herself and her family to beautiful homes, stylish clothes, and expensive automobiles, she never stopped working. She kept traveling and giving demonstrations of her hair care method, all the while opening more salons and increasing her army of hair culturists. She occasionally visited faraway places such as Cuba,

Jamaica, and Panama, and she relied heavily on Lelia and her attorneys to help with the business in her absence. Young Mae often went with her grandmother on these journeys, sometimes acting as a model during presentations.

As Walker's company grew, so did her social connections. She was suddenly making friends with respected African Americans such as W. E. B. DuBois—the same accomplished man who had inspired her in Saint Louis in 1904. Walker also caught the attention of Booker T. Washington, though it wasn't easy. In 1912, she confronted Washington because he was not going to give her a chance to speak at a meeting of the National Negro Business League (NNBL) in Chicago, Illinois. Walker stood and spoke at the meeting unannounced. She used the opportunity to express what she truly hoped to do with her money: "Now my object in life is not simply to make money for myself or to spend it on myself in dressing or running around in an automobile. But I love to use a part of what I make in trying to help others." By 1913, Washington—who ran the NNBL—formally arranged for Walker to speak at a **convention** in Philadelphia, Pennsylvania. Like so many others, he heard Walker's voice and was impressed with her drive.

Mary McLeod Bethune, a nationally recognized educator, also admired Walker and benefited from her generous spirit. Like Walker, Bethune was a child of former slaves and had been similarly determined to improve her circumstances. She ultimately founded the Daytona Educational and Industrial Training School for Negro Girls in Daytona, Florida. The school later became part of present-day Bethune-Cookman College. Walker was

Walker realized it was important to educate women of her race all over the world. One of her dreams was to found a girl's industrial training school in Africa. Though she was not able to pursue this goal in her lifetime, she left $10,000 in her will to be used toward funding such a school.

Walker celebrates the opening of a YMCA in Indianapolis.

pleased to donate money to Bethune in 1915 to assist her efforts in Florida.

Walker often reached out to the poor within her community. She frequently prepared Christmas food baskets for less-fortunate families in Indianapolis and helped support local institutions ranging from YMCAs to African American retirement facilities.

In addition, she hosted elegant parties to benefit organizations such as the National Association for the Advancement of Colored People (NAACP), which fought to end discrimination.

Because of the charity work she did close to home, the citizens of Indianapolis were devastated to see Walker move to New York in 1916. As one reporter noted, "When the needy poor and institutions are no longer cheered, inspired and helped by her timely assistance, then and not until then will we fully appreciate what she was to Indianapolis."

SUPPORTING CULTURE AND FIGHTING FOR EQUAL RIGHTS

Walker was eager to share her wealth with New York City, just as she had with Indianapolis. By 1916, she was making more than $100,000 a year. Because the value of money changes over time, that amount would be worth more than $1.5 million today. Walker used a portion of her income to back African American artists, authors, performers, politicians, and scholars in Harlem, one of the city's African American neighborhoods. The coming together of these creative minds, which blossomed into the **Harlem Renaissance**, was made possible in part because of philanthropists like Walker. She also supported passionate political groups that were calling for an end to discrimination.

While it had been 49 years since Walker was born into the cotton fields of Louisiana, in some ways little had changed in the South. Much to her horror, she realized that lynching was an ongoing problem in some areas. In May 1916, she became determined to support the NAACP's antilynching campaign when a mentally disabled teenager was killed by

a brutal mob in Robinson, Texas. Stunned by the hatred and cruelty with which the boy's attackers had acted—and perhaps remembering the violence that was said to have killed her first husband—Walker was driven to take action against both lynching and the race riots erupting in the Midwest.

She and other African American leaders headed to Washington, D.C., in 1917 with the goal of meeting with President Woodrow Wilson. Walker was convinced that the only way to end the killing was to recognize lynching and mob violence as a national crime punishable by U.S. law. Much to her disappointment, Wilson was unable to meet with the antilynching committee. Walker was not so easily ignored.

Shortly after her return from Washington, she eagerly organized the first annual Madam Walker Beauty Culturists Union Convention in Philadelphia. The event was designed to allow Walker's hair culturists to share their experiences, ranging from personal hair growth to financial success as her agents. She hoped they'd walk away with new ideas about how to shape their careers as businesswomen. But she also wanted her hair culturists to understand that it was not enough simply to make money and create personal independence. She urged the women to see the social injustices around them and to respond with determination, pride in their past, and confidence that they could help those in need.

The 28th president of the United States, Woodrow Wilson was in office from 1913 to 1921.

The Walker Union lived up to her expectations when the group addressed President Wilson in a telegram, urging him to consider antilynching legislation before further violence occurred. The president was impossible to persuade, but Walker and her union had made it clear that African American women would not stop their fight against discrimination and violence.

As 1917 drew to a close, Walker continued to support the role African Americans played in World War I (1914–1918). When she moved in 1918 to a thirty-room mansion she had built in Irvington-on-Hudson, New York, she often hosted elaborate get-togethers where both white and African American guests discussed the conflict overseas. During these parties at her new home, which Walker called Villa Lewaro (a name created from the first two letters of Lelia's full name at the time, Lelia Walker

Walker did more than just talk about African American troops at Villa Lewaro. She held herself accountable for making it clear how indebted the country was for their service. In February 1919, she told members of the entirely African American 369th Infantry to look at her home "as their own" and sponsored a two-week open house for the returning soldiers and their families.

Robinson), she voiced her pride in the African American soldiers and volunteers bravely fighting for their country.

Sadly, many of these men and women faced discrimination from white troops even while the war was raging. Walker encouraged Americans of all races to unite against the enemy, but she was quick to add that African Americans returning from the war deserved the same respect and consideration that white veterans received when they came home. The discussions that played out during the dinners at Villa Lewaro prompted both African American and white leaders to start considering how to achieve equal rights, even if it would be several more years before this goal was reached.

Walker's efforts during World War I are only a single example of how she motivated people to build a nation where everyone could share their talents, express their opinions, and experience success. Unfortunately, the woman who had pushed so hard to end discrimination was growing older, becoming ill, and fighting for more time.

CHAPTER FIVE

THE END OF A LIFE AND AN UNDYING LEGACY

*In the later years of her life, Walker wasn't
well enough to leave Villa Lewaro.*

By 1919, Walker had been suffering from kidney disease and high blood pressure for about three years. Though she had remained active despite her illness, she was finally forced to cancel several of her public appearances and travel plans as her condition worsened. The setback was frustrating

One of the main reasons Walker had worked tirelessly for decades was to provide for her daughter Lelia (above), who headed the company after Walker died.

for her, as she was anxious to continue her efforts with the antilynching movement and still owned a highly successful business.

As time passed, however, doctors advised her to leave Villa Lewaro as little as possible. Lelia and Mae were on their way back from a trip to Panama when Walker died on May 25, 1919. She was 51 years old and had kept her fiery determination right up until the final week of her life. On May 19, she spoke the following words before losing consciousness: "I want to live to help my race."

REMEMBERING HER PUSH FOR PROGRESS

People all over the world took note of Walker's death, and she was mourned by men and women, rich and poor, whites and African Americans. Recognized in an Associated Press newspaper story as "the wealthiest negro woman in the United States, if not the entire world," the daughter of former slaves never forgot to show generosity to the people who needed it most. Indeed, before she died, Walker willed part of her fortune to the charity organizations and social efforts she had supported during her lifetime.

Lelia, who later changed her name to A'Lelia, became president of the Madam C. J. Walker Manufacturing Company after her mother's death. A'Lelia died in 1931. In 1985, the company was sold to Indianapolis businessman Ray Randolph. Both Villa Lewaro and the business's original headquarters in Indianapolis are considered **National Historic Landmarks**, though Walker's home is now privately owned and not open to the public. In 2001, Walker's great-great-granddaughter, A'Lelia Bundles, published a biography of her famous relative titled *On Her Own Ground: The Life and Times of Madam C. J. Walker*.

Walker was famous for not giving up simply because things got tough, and that didn't change during the last few months of her life. Despite her bad health, she was never too tired to promote social justice, and she frequently spoke with leaders from her favorite charities and campaigns even after she found it hard to leave Villa Lewaro. "I am not going to die," she sometimes said during this period, "because I have so much work to do yet."

Completed in 1918, Villa Lewaro has vaulted ceilings and marble staircases.

Though it was several years after Walker's death before African Americans were legally granted equal rights, her determination and personal achievements forced people to realize the possibility and need for change. Walker became an entrepreneur and activist during an era when African American women were often slaves in all but name, laboring tirelessly in kitchens and farm fields but rarely escaping poverty and discrimination. She helped her customers feel more confident about how they looked and the careers they could create if they fought to make their dreams come true. As she once commented, "If I have accomplished anything in life, it is because I have been willing to work hard."

Walker's hard work paid off in ways she could never have imagined. The self-made millionaire demonstrated that people who are poor and treated unfairly can improve their lives, and she was a living example that wealth and success should be used to aid others.

Life & Career Skills

The people who attended Walker's funeral represented the wide range of individuals who benefited from her generous spirit and who were amazed by her accomplishments—reflecting her extraordinary ability to connect with people. Mourners included Walker sales agents, government officials, real estate agents, architects, composers, publishers, attorneys, doctors, social activists, journalists, and entertainers. She is buried in Woodlawn Cemetery in New York City.

Timeline

1867　Sarah Breedlove is born on December 23 in Delta, Louisiana.

ca. 1873　Sarah's mother, Minerva Breedlove, dies.

ca. 1875　Sarah's father, Owen Breedlove, dies.

1878　Sarah moves to Vicksburg, Mississippi, with her sister, Louvenia.

1881　Sarah marries Moses McWilliams.

1885　Sarah gives birth to Lelia McWilliams (who later changes her first name to A'Lelia) on June 6.

1888　McWilliams is possibly involved in a race riot or lynching and dies.

1889　Sarah and Lelia move to Saint Louis, Missouri.

1894　Sarah marries John Davis on August 11.

mid-1890s　Sarah begins to lose her hair.

1902　Lelia starts attending classes at Knoxville College in Knoxville, Tennessee.

1903　In November, Sarah ends her relationship with Davis. She begins selling hair care products for Annie Turnbo.

1904　Saint Louis hosts the World's Fair as well as several famous African Americans and members of the National Association of Colored Women (NACW).

1905　In July, Sarah moves to Denver, Colorado, where she will ultimately perfect her own version of a scalp treatment to cure hair loss.

1906　Sarah marries Charles Joseph "C. J." Walker in January.

mid-1906　Madam C. J. Walker starts advertising Madam Walker's Wonderful Hair Grower and begins traveling across Colorado to promote her product.

1907   Walker leaves Denver and travels through Oklahoma, Texas, Kansas, Arkansas, Louisiana, Mississippi, and Alabama to give demonstrations and spread the word about her hair grower. She earns $3,652 in sales.

1908   Walker settles in Pittsburgh, Pennsylvania, and she and Lelia establish Lelia College.

1910   Walker moves to Indianapolis, Indiana, and opens a factory there.

1911   Walker officially creates the Madam C. J. Walker Manufacturing Company in Indiana.

1912   Walker's marriage to C. J. ends in divorce, and Lelia adopts a 13-year-old named Mae.

1913   Walker is making more than $3,000 a month and purchases an elegant home in New York City.

1913–1916   Walker continues to expand her business and travels to countries including Cuba, Jamaica, and Panama. She also starts building her reputation as a philanthropist who makes major financial contributions to groups and causes benefiting African Americans. By 1916, she is making more than $100,000 a year and officially moves to New York City.

1917   Walker heads to Washington, D.C., with other African American leaders in the hopes of speaking to President Woodrow Wilson about antilynching legislation. Shortly after her return, she organizes the first annual Madam Walker Beauty Culturists Union Convention in Philadelphia, Pennsylvania.

1918   Walker moves to Villa Lewaro in Irvington-on-Hudson, New York.

1919   Walker dies on May 25 at the age of fifty-one.

GLOSSARY

convention (kuhn-VEN-shuhn) a large, formal meeting or gathering

correspondence class (kor-uh-SPON-dens KLASS) a class where students receive instruction through materials delivered in the mail, instead of in a classroom

cultivating (KUHL-tuh-vay-teeng) developing by studying

discrimination (DISS-krim-i-NAY-shuhn) unequal treatment of a person that is often based on gender, religion, or race

entrepreneur (ON-truh-pruh-NUR) someone who starts a new business

Harlem Renaissance (HAHR-luhm REN-uh-sahnss) a period in American history during the 1920s and 1930s when African American art, literature, entertainment, and social activism flourished in New York City

industry (IN-duh-stree) the act of making goods and services for sale

lynched (LINCH-d) killed by a mob (often by hanging) without the authority of the law

marketing (MAR-ki-teeng) selling a product or promoting that product to increase sales

National Historic Landmarks (NA-shu-nuhl hiss-TOR-ik LAND-marks) buildings, structures, or areas that the U.S. government formally declares to have played an important role in American history

ointment (OINT-muhnt) a type of medicine that is often applied to the skin

philanthropist (fuh-LAN-thruh-pist) a person who uses his or her time and money to help others

riot (RYE-uht) public violence or disorder

segregation (seg-ruh-GAY-shuhn) a situation in which separate treatment or opportunities are given to people based on their gender, religion, or race

sharecroppers (SHAIR-krah-purs) farmers who rent the land they work on and usually pay the owner with a portion of their crops

For More Information

Books

Aller, Susan Bivin. *Madam C. J. Walker.* Minneapolis: Lerner Publications Company, 2007.

Krohn, Katherine E. *Madam C. J. Walker: Pioneer Businesswoman.* Mankato, MN.: Capstone Press, 2006.

Nichols, Catherine. *Madam C. J. Walker.* Danbury, CT: Children's Press, 2005.

Web Sites

Madam C. J. Walker: The Official Web Site
www.madamecjwalker.com/
Includes an interactive timeline and many images

National Park Service: Villa Lewaro
www.cr.nps.gov/nr/travel/pwwmh/ny22.htm
For a brief biography of Madam C. J. Walker and information about the stately mansion she built in New York

The Schomburg Center for Research in Black Culture: Madame C. J. Walker (Sarah Breedlove)
www.si.umich.edu/chico/Harlem/text/cjwalker.html
Features information about Walker and the company within the context of Harlem from 1900 to 1940

INDEX

ABOUT THE AUTHOR

Katie Marsico worked as an editor in children's publishing before she began writing her own reference books. She lives with her husband, Carl, daughter, Maria, and son, C. J., in a suburb of Chicago, Illinois. Ms. Marsico is grateful to her friends and colleagues E. Russell Primm and Pam Rosenberg for helping her get her start as a children's author and for giving her the opportunity to write this book.